CHARACTER
HOW TO STRENGTHEN IT

❧

FUNK & WAGNALLS COMPANY
Publishers
NEW YORK AND LONDON

MENTAL EFFICIENCY SERIES

CHARACTER
HOW TO STRENGTHEN IT

By D. STARKE

Translated by Lorenzo O'Rourke, M.A.

AUTHORIZED EDITION

"He who can control himself can easily master events and man"

PUBLISHED BY BROWNSTONE BOOKS

PREFACE

To SAMUEL SMILES the crown and glory of life was Character. It is the noblest possession of man, constituting a rank in itself, and an estate in the general good-will, dignifying every station, and exalting every position in society. Of itself Character is power and influence. Experience has taught us that the worth and the strength of a state depend upon the character of its men rather than on the form of its institutions. Just as the letters of the alphabet enable us to spell *reputation,* so do the actions, looks, and words of a man enable us to read his true *character.* Character is what one is; reputation is what one is thought to be. A man's character being himself must be molded by himself alone. In this work the Author, taking as his motto, "The man who can master himself can easily control events and man," teaches his readers how to strengthen character. He does this by explaining what constitutes strength of character, what this wonderful power can achieve, and how it may be acquired and utilized to best advantage.

Schopenhauer, whose cynical criticism gives voice to the bitterness of his heart against the world's whole artificial life, found time to teach us that men best show their character in trifles when they are not on their guard. "It is in insignificant matters," said he, "and in the simplest habits, that we often see the boundless egotism which pays no regard to the feelings of others, and denies nothing to itself." All the petty vexations of life serve their purpose in training us in moral discipline; these provide the severest test of character. There are many men who could face great dangers with calmness and resignation, yet who, if they be taken off their guard and their will be opposed, or their efforts thwarted, fly into uncontrollable passion. A man of character never allows the sun to set on his wrath, nor does he permit it to rise on his temerity. In these pages one is taught by a master-hand how the appetites and passions must be controlled to develop that calm force which is a factor necessary to self-domination, and how such physical ills as may arise from nervous affections, enervating forces, fear, etc., are to be overcome.

Nothing is left to chance. The body must be brought into harmony with the mind in every

effort made to acquire patience and perseverance. Exercises for the development, both tem-
peramental and physical, of character are provided in separate series. Impulsiveness of
thought leads to impulsiveness of action; therefore, the reader is taught to control his impulses; to check irritability; and to cultivate
that calm which permits one to concentrate one's
powers, to use them advantageously in moments
of excitement and stress. The exercises are
designed to impart the quality of endurance,
which is the keystone of character.

In the pages that follow, the Author leads the
reader along the way he must travel to achieve
success. The man who succeeds is he who saw
his object in early life and never lost sight of it.
"Genius," Bulwer tells us, "is but fine observation strengthened by fixity of purpose."
Every man who is stedfastly resolute and a
vigilant observer can attain success. Strength
of character is resolution. Resolve to do something, and it will be done. Napoleon once said,
"The truest wisdom is a resolute determination." The man of strong character is he who
achieves success in business. His forcefulness
is sustained by foresight, prudence, discernment, reason, logic, and clear thinking.

In the home, where one must learn to bear
and forbear, strength of character is indispensable. There egotism invariably rules. Individual comfort is always in direct ratio to the
efforts put forth to acquire it. We all seek
some end, and to attain it must submit ourselves
to the necessary discipline. There is need for
strict attention to little things, for on these
depend much of the peace and harmony of life.
The man of strong will applies all the energies
of his body and mind to every task that he ·
undertakes and so avoids that failure which
besets his weaker associates.

In business the one great difference between
men—between the weak and the strong, the
mean and the mighty—is one of character.
It is not what a man makes but what a man does
that he should give thought to. Let him think
first of his character and then of his circumstances; for, character attracts but circumstances
are dependent upon it. Some men, by combin-
ing great abilities with promising circumstances,
have not only succeeded in acquiring distinction,
but in creating characters that are the envy and
admiration of mankind. Given a strong character, and energy, determination, and a fixt purpose will be found to attend it. These are the

qualities that enable us to develop mentally, morally, and physically; that compel us to surmount all obstacles, to overcome all difficulties; and, finally, that teach us to resist temptation, and to bear the heaviest burdens cheerfully; the qualities that bring calmness before the storm, and fearlessness in the face of danger. He who heeds the advice given in the following pages will learn not only that character controls fame and fortune, but also that only the man who is master of himself can exercise a governing influence over his fellow men.

THE PUBLISHERS.

CONTENTS

ix

PART TWO

CHARACTER: HOW TO DEVELOP IT FOR
BUSINESS AND DAILY LIFE

PART I
CHARACTER: ITS ACQUISITION AND MASTERY

CHAPTER I

WHAT CONSTITUTES STRENGTH OF CHARACTER

STRENGTH of character consists of an *ensemble* of qualities which endows its possessor with illimitable power over his instincts and his passions. It is the mastery of self at its highest expression: the application of the power of will to the multiplicity of temptations which constantly assail us. Further, it is the emancipation of the mind from the prejudices which enslave feeble souls, disdain for the petty annoyances whose repetition wears away an intermittent energy.

Strength of character aids us to elicit acts of the will with freedom, at the same time enabling us to bear up under reverses as well as to realize what we set out to accomplish. It is strength of character which enables us to consummate the act that we have fixt our choice upon; and thanks to it we not only can proceed surely in the choice of our resolutions, but are also equipped with the means to persevere in them.

At no former period whatsoever has strength of character been so indispensable as it is at the present time. Education, more widely diffused than ever, has refined human aspirations, given great scope to ambition, made more bitter the struggle for wealth. All feel themselves called, but how many are chosen? The world is filled with people who complain of their luck, instead of inquiring into its causes, while humbly admitting that it proceeds from frivolity and weakness. Anarchy of motive, giving in at the first impulse, hate of effort, concur to bring about defeat after defeat, and discouragement does the rest.

It is difficult to keep a foothold on a declivity; nevertheless, when one is sure of his way and determined to climb, he will reach the summit in spite of all obstacles. On the other hand, he, who instead of putting all his strength to the gripping of the rough ledges that might aid his ascent, permits himself to slip back without resistance, is pretty sure to roll to the bottom—lucky, indeed, if his fall be not fatal.

The obstacles we meet with are nothing less than our lower instincts, which disable us when we have not the strength to surmount them.

Strength of character is not a simple thing: it is the resultant of a complex effort to exert the will directed upon a single point—the mastery of self. We should, then, extend pity to the weak ones to whom we have just alluded, and who, alas, are legion; and at the same time we should seek to convince them of the truth.

Now, their principal defect consists in giving the preponderance to emotion over reason. They never make use of the will for the purpose of reflection; but finding themselves going wrong they bring their instincts into play: "I am wrong it is true, but what would you have? I was made that way and I can not make myself over again." By declaring their conviction of the immovability of character they think to acquit themselves of the faults of fancy or momentary humor. They pretend that they are not able to change the character of the motives which are the foundation of volition in what concerns their habitual faults, and with this erroneous premise they allow themselves to go ahead, with a deplorable lack of all resistance.

It is true that we rarely succeed in com-

II.2

pletely transforming our nature, but through strength of character we succeed in neutralizing its manifestations up to the point where we no longer suffer from the exaggerations caused by ill-represt impulsiveness. It is only by self-restraint that we succeed in avoiding the error which impels us to obey the promptings of the moment, and thus condemns us to moral frailty and inconsistence.

The stereotyped saying that man is the slave of his passions has grown old only in appearance: it is as good as ever.

He who does not feel in himself the strength that character gives, must forego the triumph which comes from enfranchising oneself from irrational impulses.

The term "passions," which embraces inordinate, even sensual, appetites, is, perhaps, a little too pompous to apply to the daily inclinations and trivial acts which are suggested to us by weak character. But one should guard against making the mistake of those who only attach importance to great sentiments. Life is composed of a thousand little resolutions which, taken separately, may seem puerile enough, but combined form a formidable sheaf. Atrophy of will with regard to the envisaging of life is at

the present time more than mere waste; it is a
vice and an obstacle, something void in law.

We have now arrived at a point in education
which permits a more detailed conception of
moral personality. Social life is a field of labor
for all, rich and poor alike, to whom indolence
is repugnant. It is a field of action for each
one.

For the poor it is a question of getting rich.
For the rich it is a question of keeping what
they have got.

You may say, perhaps, there are those who
are modest and wise enough to be content with
their lot; and this is possibly true as far as
the second group is concerned, but if we admit
it of the first we should have to include both
under the denomination of the wise.

Let us remark, moreover, that both qualifications are embraced in the same category;
there is no difference between a man who is
satisfied with his lot and a sage. To be content
with one's lot indicates strength of character
of a very uncommon order. It implies a
natural appreciation of one's own value, and at
the same time self-sufficing strength without the
need of foreign support or protection. To acquire this type of wisdom, however, excessive

firmness of will is implied. This is the reason
why we should include the modest, those *content
with their lot,* and the wise as well, in the too-
thin ranks of the army of the apostles of character.

What remain are the modest without further
qualifications, and of these we shall have something to say. In the great social struggle that
is going on he who keeps aloof is a shirker or a
coward. He that shuns the combat must forego the triumph. It is only the militant who
have a right to the joy of victory. The modest
who are not also wise belong to the timid sort,
a prey to all the ills of their defect; they conceal themselves under an appearance of disdain
which is only too frequently a mask to conceal
envious traits. The really modest struggle on
in silence, without parade; but they take care
to hold themselves aloof from the fracas and
contribute, as do the wise, to the upbuilding of
progress.

Character, therefore, is the resultant of an
effort of will directed at itself. And, to acquire
the power of manipulating, of "canalizing" this
power of will, mastery of oneself is presup-
posed. If we would really dominate others it is
indispensable that we gain the mastery over our-

selves; and to arrive at this end we should begin
by defining the nature of this force, so superior
to others that make more noise but lack its solid
value.

Self-mastery is a quality of the will that permits us to choose with reflection the act that
we wish to accomplish. It is the power of
directing its proper actions to their rightful
aim, while at the same time freeing them from
all foreign preoccupations. More than this, it
is above all that which gives us the power to
rid ourselves of foreign suggestions.

By the word "foreign" we further mean the
conquering of other than the motives opposed to
the resolution we have fixt upon. The domi-
nation that one submits to nearly always has
its source in the egoism of our neighbor, whose
views are different from ours. It is a rare
thing when egoism is not paramount as the
vital sentiment, urging upon others those things
which are to our advantage. Rarely do counsellors yield to an impulse devoid of the element
of personality: it is always in their own interest,
tho sometimes unconsciously, that they seek to
impose their will upon others.

There are certain persons who know so well
how to set off their insinuations that they pre-

sent them without showing any particular interest, dwelling merely on the least, but all the while directing them toward the path that seems most propitious for the accomplishments of the secret desire.

Now the man without power of will, his very existence depending on the will of others, is glad to find in the latter that pretext for decision which he finds wanting in himself.

Supposing that the givers of advice are clever and dishonest; persons without strength of character will be no more in their hands than so many jumping-jacks, of which their intriguers pull the strings making their plaything perform easily the acts that they can not or dare not perform themselves.

Foreign suggestions do not always come from without. They are sometimes inspired by divergent thoughts which, starting out from the subject that we are studying, gradually get so far away from them that we have to make a considerable effort of thought to get back to the genesis of their formation. Now feeble minds are incapable of this effort, and they yield to the consideration of ideas at first parasitical, then alien, whose sloping road leads them to a *terrain* that they had no intention of treading.

Such persons are like those who, having set out to follow the course of a river, allow themselves, for lack of direction, to be led into adjacent canals and, from inertia and lack of resolution, allow themselves to drift along careless of the consequence.

It happens, perchance, that the excursions are not lacking in charm, that this vagabondage confined by two changing shores may not be devoid of momentary pleasures; but when it should be time to reach the destination there is no port in sight, and the eye searches for it in vain.

This negative result is always the one reached by the weak, who allow themselves to be drawn on by ideas incompatible with those to which they naturally should have recourse.

The worst of it is that these thoughts, always determining acts and not being sufficiently developed, are generally tainted with incoherence. Reason made to rule over acts and lacking a *terrain* propitious for its development, there results from this insufficiency a propensity to do certain things the effects of which can not be foreseen. In this state of things there is reason to be thankful if the resolution, due entirely to the impulse of the moment, does not come to convert these acts into irreparable errors.

All such catastrophes can be avoided by the man who knows how to govern himself.

Such a one enlarges life by opposing to adverse events that strength which is resident in himself, and which constitutes an element powerful enough to make the struggle, at first an equal one, finally yield in his favor.

The phrase "the struggle for life" has been abused, modernists using the neologism to baptize those who put it into practise "strugglers for life." There is no need of translating the term, since all the world understands it to mean the fight that is going on for existence. Unfortunately, this is not a metaphor; it may be admitted in its literal sense. The struggle that is going on between man and matter is a real one. From prehistoric times, when our remote ancestors had to combat the elements and the beasts of primeval forests, we have changed in appearance, not in reality. The end pursued by each for the purpose of conserving his own and his family's existence—what is it but the daily prey of old? It no longer takes the form of a combat with a wild beast, but appears to us in the aspect of a hundred things essential to life, things that our activity and cleverness must overcome. The motives and the aims which animate the peaceable employee in an office are the same as those which haunted the dark thoughts of prehistoric man.

To assure oneself the means of living and of embellishing life—this is the aim of all of a man's acts. Life is a struggle; but a harmonious life of the noble type is a triumph.

Consider the successful, who, urged on in the attainment of their goal, hardly turn aside to count the victims they abandon in their path. Perhaps this indifference will be branded by strict morality, but it must be kept in mind that the victims are always the feeble, those who could not fight, and lacked even the energy to steer clear of a course too dangerous for their weak equipment.

Not to be of the weak; that is the all-important thing, all is summed up in it. Man must tend toward perfection. To surpass himself will always be the objective of the man who has not been satiated by the triumph of a day.

All great inventions have made victims.

All institutions have their martyrology; the social mechanism wills it so. There is not a single discovery whose mighty results have not been accomplished by individual misfortunes.

Things really great stand on a plane above
these contingencies.

Man must follow this model: He ought himself to be good, and his motives, as well as the
end which he has in view, ought to be worthy
ones. Too often good and evil intermingle in
the achieved result, and at times it is difficult to
differentiate between them. This is why character is indispensable to the man who would
succeed. He will take every means to acquire
it and to augment the sum of energy at its
disposal. He will force himself to distinguish
the means he employs, and to contemn unworthy
ones. Finally, in cultivating self-mastery he
will succeed not only in attaining to it, but it
will radiate from him till it reaches those who
surround him and even distant things, all of
which he will know how to turn to his own
interest and make part of his triumphal train.

CHAPTER II

CALMNESS IN STRENGTH

MAN is not always master of his feelings; that is to say, it does not always depend upon himself whether or not the solution of a given problem shall rest upon reason alone. But he is master of his acts, or, rather, he will be master of his acts from the moment he determines not to conclude upon anything until the element of character intervenes to dictate his decision. One can hardly prevent himself from having feelings; but if such belong to those classed as blamable, the law that should govern him who aims at self-control is this: Do not do that act which you are called upon the justify.

Actions are only the sanction of an emotion that seeks to affirm itself.

Persons of frail character are not sufficiently impregnated with this principle. Powerless to unravel the chaos of sensations, they allow themselves to become entangled in their mazes, merely emphasizing such acts as illustrate them and render their suppression more difficult.

25

It is always difficult, and at times impossible, not to yield to those feelings which have become a sort of habit of the soul; but each one can suppress their manifestation, especially if they clash with the laws of common sense and morality.

Supposing you are a miser, you can not escape a disagreeable impression at the sight of money being spent; but this propensity, examined calmly and represt by the reasonableness which comes from strength of character, becomes a simple trait of wise economy.

There is not one passion which may not, under the influence of a salutary wish, divest itself of its blamable features, and take in a certain quality of sentiment.

"The passions, for the most part," as has been said elsewhere, "take root in a sentiment worthy of praise. There is a passion which, like evil in the fable, spreads terror everywhere, and which the people in their picturesque language call a pest; it is envy, the result of moral suffering, which, pushed to the point of paroxysm, produces psychical conditions bordering on aberration. None the less, if we go back to the genesis of this leprosy of the soul, we shall find a sentiment quite noble, namely, emulation, which is born of the desire to become the equal of those who have distinguished themselves in some branch of science, or won applause by their success."

And further on, the theme is pursued:

"Take prodigality, an extremely dissolute passion. Never has a prodigal known success. Abundant harvests will never be his, for, according to the familiar saying, 'He eats his wheat from the stalk.' Reaping-time comes, but no one ever finds in the prodigal's field more than an ear or two of corn, left from the wastage of the harvest. Now this vice is nothing more nor less than the amplification of something that one can not admire enough; it is the exaggeration of unreasonable generosity which produces the spendthrift."

It is thus apparent that precious qualities can be changed into reprehensible passions, and that it is possible to mold faults into solid virtues —if only we know how to develop the necessary force of character. And one of the indispensable conditions for maintaining the *milieu* from which character must spring is calmness, without which no serious resolution can be worked out.

It is not in the heat of enthusiasm that ideas

are fertilized. Unreasonable enthusiasm is generally sterile, since it always strikes a note that it can not maintain. It is impossible to prolong an infatuation, and still more difficult to exploit it with unflagging ardor. There are many reasons for this; first of all, the satiety produced by habit, which, by attenuating emotion, does not permit us to exteriorize it with uniform intensity; little by little repetition comes to annul it, rendering its manifestation painful and soon impossible. Thus, it often happens that an idea adopted with excessive fervor may be dropt before our enthusiasm and quick-succeeding satiety have permitted us to give it the consideration it merits.

Another reason is the levity with which so many adopt a proposition, governed entirely by the excitement of the moment of its conception. They plunge forward without looking ahead, and are halted by the first obstacles, repulsed and disenchanted. If necessity forces them to persevere, it is with bad grace that they set themselves to the task, without any of the necessary conditions of success, all having been sacrificed to their stupidity. Finally, it is difficult for enthusiasts to detach their attention from diverse objects of which they perceive only

the attractive sides; and the infatuation that
takes possession of them at sight of a new idea
always has the effect of attenuating that caused
by the preceding idea. From this scattering
of energy must result merely efforts without
appreciable result, and the too-eager aspirant, if
lucky enough to escape defeat, is condemned
to a kind of half-success.

How much more enviable are those who submit to the law of calmness, which permits of
singleness of purpose, and may be classified as
a proof of strength. Calmness, in this sense, is
a state of quietude which enables us to reas-
semble our divergent thoughts and meditate
with profit. It is always the index of power.
For, while debility and stupidity squander their
strength in sterile demonstrations, calmness engenders contemplation which gives to ideas of
promise an opportunity to take form and develop.

Without calmness, strength of character could
never exist. Calmness is a faculty which fights
sentiment with sentiment. It is the mobilizing
of energy, and its concentration upon the point
which seems to us the most worthy of consideration. It is a sort of crystalization of passion
into an intense desire to come to grips with

that which seems most promising of results. It is by calmness alone that we can acquire freedom of mind, the root of unity of action which permits of activity, coordinate and complete.

Calmness is not the foe of the feelings; it is their regulator. Thanks to it, resolutions made outside the domain of caprice are not at the mercy of fancy's every wind. Calmness is a power, since it rejects all emotion, all excitation, which might prove an obstacle to clear and enlightened reflection. It releases us from the vassalage of fugitive impressions, and enables us to rid ourselves of all except the desired object.

Who has not smiled at the sight of a poodle raging at a huge mastiff? The pug attacks the Molossian from all sides—makes desperate leaps at his head, gnaws at his legs, barking furiously. The big dog contents himself with lifting his snout out of the reach of the cur's attacks, and, undisturbed by the latter's howls, would turn aside to avoid him; but this being impossible by reason of the annoyer's importunity, a mighty paw is at length lifted over the cur's fragile frame, and the ridiculous adversary takes to flight howling, giving in at the first blow in a struggle that promised to be a furious one.

For those who like to make deductions from things, and to look upon the humblest events as lessons, there is much to learn from this simple incident. When one knows he is strong he will not waste his strength in useless actions. He will let his adversary exhaust himself in ludicrous assaults, reflecting the while upon the definitive act which will put an end to the contest.

Calmness is the appanage of energy; it is the attitude of those who, conscious of their strength, have no desire to squander it in sterile efforts to prove its existence to themselves. It is impossible to attain to strength of character unless one, at the same time, enforces himself to calmness, which is the generator of the active resolution, the fulcrum of achievement.

"A dullard," says an Arabian philosopher, "once carelessly set his house on fire, whereupon by his frantic efforts to extinguish the flames he made the fire spread the more.

"The wise man will take all necessary precautions against fire, but if it breaks out, instead of precipitating himself into the midst of it with hasty, futile efforts, he will call calmness to his aid, and it will suggest to him the means to employ. When he has fixt on these he will employ them without so much as a useless gesture,

and to such good effect that the time given to
calm reflection will be made up a hundredfold
by the coherence and appropriateness of the
acts suggested.''

The moral of this apolog may be applied to
all the acts of life. It is a question of putting
a bridle upon imprudence, and of calling to our
aid in grave circumstances calm self-possession,
thus bringing about the solution which never
will suggest itself to a mind in the effervescence
of emotion.

We can not repeat this often enough; calmness is the sign of strength, an element of
victory. And what finer victory can be hoped
for than a triumph over passions which belittle
us and deprive us of the means of success?

The struggle is not presented to all under the
same aspect. Certain vehement spirits find it
harder to attain to calmness than do more
apathetic ones. And in this connection we can
not put sufficient emphasis upon the difference
between calmness and apathy.

Superficial persons have a too-pronounced
tendency to confound the two states. Calmness
does not exclude energy; far from that, it often
represents it. It is the mark of real strength.
It is also the characteristic sign of self-mastery.

Without calmness strength of character can not be really manifested, since it is calmness alone which exercises rule over virile resolutions. It is sometimes said that calmness is, above all, a mark of resignation. Sometimes it involves a condition of things which doubles the power of action. In whatever phase, calmness is a state of mind, willed and chosen.

Apathy, on the contrary, is a kind of involuntary negligence; we do not hanker for it, but we submit to it. The apathetic are those whose sensations are seldom manifested; their sufferings, like their joys, are of an attenuated sort, or, at least, seem so; for the apathetic are sometimes simply the lazy. These last suffer as much as the sensitive, but their hate of all exertion prevents them from getting any relief in their suffering. They prefer to bear it in its entirety rather than risk the effort that might ameliorate it. The power of character will ever remain unknown to them, and all their life long they will be the plaything of circumstances which they will never have the will-power to control.

We see what an abyss separates apathy from calmness; the first depresses, the second brings comfort.

Calmness it is which permits reason to dictate decisions of importance, and, thanks to calmness, strength of character may reach development and extend its influence to each one of our acts.

In the course of this work we shall speak of the means of attaining to this precious trait of character—a trait which permits us to be masters of ourselves, so that we may read ourselves like an open book.

"Know thyself," says the sage. And we may add: "Cultivate calmness of mind, which will provide the field for putting this knowledge to profit."

CHAPTER III

PHYSICAL PAIN AND THE POWER OF CHARACTER

By reason of its invincible robustness character is able to exert an influence of the happiest, surest kind upon physical sensations. Between the mind and the body there exists an incontestable solidarity which subjects the latter to the environment determined by the moral state. We will not enlarge upon the correlation of moral impressions and physical sensations.

Every one knows that imaginary maladies are found, not only among victims of hyper-neurosis, but also among many people of sane mind whose only fault it is to give free rein to their imagination upon the appearance of the slightest illness. There is then produced a sort of suggestion which passes from the brain to the part affected, the least symptoms of pain being thus heightened.

An old physician once said to a young woman who was complaining of various troubles for

which she asked of him a remedy: "Don't think
of them; it is the most powerful of all cures."

The two active elements, physical and moral,
are then so intimately intertwined that to think
of pain is enough to aggravate it. There is no
need, however, of referring to these trivial
cases; we will consider one in which the malady
is not at all a question of nervousness. We will
admit that it exists really, undubitably, and is
neither the work of an excited imagination, nor
of weakness degenerating into mean and selfish
fear. In this case there is no use in saying, like
the physician: "Don't think about it any more."
Such a resolve would be puerile, because of its
impossibility and knowledge that it is an empty
formula. Nevertheless, we have before our eyes
every day the example of people who, tho suffering from a definite malady, can forget all
about it when their minds are occupied by something of importance that does not allow them
to dwell upon their physical condition except as
a secondary consideration.

"I knew a man," relates B. Dangennes,
"who was suffering from an acute form of
neuralgia, which compelled him to keep in bed
in a room of utter darkness during the hours
the sickness was torturing him. He held that

every movement aggravated the pain, and re-
fused to make any effort. One day, when the
crisis was at its height, a servant burst into the
room with the news that an accident had happened to the patient's little son, who was then
brought in with a broken arm. Mastered by
emotion, the father got right up, sent for the
doctor, and gave all necessary directions. When
the arm was reset, the child comforted, and the
father sought to regain his bed, it dawned upon
him that during this whole time he had given
hardly a thought to the suffering which had
excluded everything else from his mind. Struck
with amazement at the proof that painful suffering might be diminished by occupying oneself with something entirely foreign from it, he
decided to start anew from that day. He made
more and more effort, humored his neuralgia
less, and finally felt the pain decrease and even
had intervals of complete relief.''

We have similar examples, on a smaller scale,
before our eyes every day, and may, if we are
in good faith, actually prove in our own persons
the truth of this observation. It is, then, the
part of wisdom to create the diversion which is
supplied to us by some emotion, whose vibra-
tions, by producing in the brain a vital move-

ment, result in a tension foreign to that of the physical pain.

We have here the triumph of strength of character.

History is filled with examples which serve to prove that physical pain can be decreased by effort of will to divert the human mind into opposite channels. Posidonius said in the midst of sufferings caused by a grave sickness: "In order to forget my suffering, and prove my contempt for it, I find it good to discourse upon pain in general, and what I feel of it does not prevent me of speaking of it to some purpose."

Have we not all read episodes of the death of the martyrs, wherein it is told how they suffered the worst tortures with amazing serenity? How some of them, escaping death, declared that their attitude was not the pride that would foil the torturer of the joy of tasting the anguish of his victims, but was the effort of will that transported them into that heaven which they had the conviction that they would conquer for themselves. The foretaste of the vision of Paradise gave them, then, the power to conceive so strongly of the paradisiacal joys as to produce in them a moral tension the intensity of which made them forget physical torture.

Do we not, indeed, see much nearer at hand, men and women who abandon the flowery existence which might be theirs, for the joy of sacrifice? They give up their freedom, sleep on a board, eat in small quantities what would not satisfy a pauper, suffer cold, seek no surety for the future, and yet experience not the multiplied sufferings that all this would seem to portend, but a plenitude of well-being which makes them forget cold, hunger, and loss of liberty. They are animated, like the ancient martyrs, by an idea whose obsession has become a source of strength; the joys of the future which they call eternity makes the rod that leads to it seem sweet. Without, however, taking up the cult of mysticism, it is given to each one of us to lessen bodily pain by making use of some preoccupation that will have weight enough to act to advantage upon physical impressions. One hears something like this every minute without being struck with the banality of it: "If I did not have to do such or such a thing I wouldn't have got up, such is my headache."

If it be desirable to go further in this matter of evoking before the mind deductive examples of this kind, here are two: On one hand a man is lowered into his bed suffering a martyrdom which is increased by the accumulation of his thoughts, all converging upon his physical condition. He can neither read nor speak, but keeps up a continual *tête à tête* with his sickness, which is the only means of combat left to him by his cerebral inaction.

The other picture is that of a man intent in the midst of his sufferings upon the thought of the necessity of leaving his bed. This thought engenders a resolution; and, while it is taking form, he forces himself to ignore his pain which, moreover, had already begun to absorb his exclusive attention. With the decision to get up and go out comes the wish to make the necessary movements to accomplish the act. This wish gives birth to a desire to get better, which undergoes such rapid development as to suggest the power of acting, just as if he were already well. Our man, helpless and inert a moment ago, surmounts his weakness and is already at his toilet preparatory to going out. He is now in the street and his *amour propre* takes a hand; to look ill and wretched is repugnant to him; he braces up, and his preoccupation in making a good appearance diminishes the effects of his illness. Finally, the thought of the walk by degrees takes the place of the thought of his malady. To be sure, he suffers still, but this suffering has become purely physical; the brain no longer furnishes it new nourishment, and at times he forgets about it altogether. Finally, the moment arrives to accomplish the object of his setting out; his whole attention is concentrated upon the words he is to use, the arguments he is to put forward upon. which will depend an acceptance or refusal, in short all the consequences of his act.

His headache has already become less racking; the truce granted to the ruling idea of suffering has done its work; this latter train of thought being diverted, moral tension canalized toward another object alters the act which is taking place in the centers of motivity, and only the throb of physical pain is felt dully by the brain. We do not here intend to enter the domain of scientific exposition, which lies beyond the range of this book, but every one knows the power of suggestion when it is applied according to the rules of rigorous research.

From all this, then, the necessary deduction is that the force that resides in character can be applied to sickness with efficacious results.

We do not say that it suppresses illness, but in cases not of fatal nature it makes the patient almost forget his malady for a time, enabling him to endure its graver phases by momentarily doing away with much of the suffering.

This effort of the will is well known to actors, who make use of it on the stage to transform themselves into the character they impersonate, giving the audience the illusion of reality, altho a few moments before they may have been suffering from some violent pain. What, for instance, is more painful than a jumping-toothache? Like headache, it is an evil that leaves others smiling and skeptical. Nevertheless, it makes the sufferer incapable of dissembling. Now, I have it on the word of many actors that none of them ever felt upon the stage the agonizing pain that it produces. We are speaking, of course, of real actors, those who have felt "the sacred fire." I have known them a few minutes before their entrance to walk their dressing-room, distrait, devoting their suffering to all the demons, in despair at the thought that it is impossible for them to appear. But at the voice of the call-boy they have instantly braced up, made a desperate draught upon the forces of character, and, despising the pain which a mo-

ment before prostrated them, appeared before
the audience, their faces the same as ever. And
for the most part there is no need of their
troubling themselves so much, for the relief so
dearly wished for nearly always comes. Nevertheless, the age of miracles has gone by, and they
find that the pain they got rid of while they were
on the stage returns on their exit.

This is a proof, you will say, that these great
manifestations of the power of character are
too transitory to be really salutary. No. For
the number of those who have to call upon them
frequently is limited enough, while those are
legion who know how to put pain to sleep by
a worthier kind of preoccupation. Study is a
most salutary means to employ. The savant
who devotes his life to important research looks
upon suffering as a negligible quantity so long
as it does not interfere with his work. If it
gets too hard to bear, it is still in his familiar
tasks that he will seek temporary oblivion.

It is, then, indispensable for all who endure
bodily pain that they call to the rescue the
strength that comes of character, and this will
enable them to weigh the means of opposing
this enemy of a redoubtable adversary,
whether under the form of a desired

object, a responsibility, or some wished-for
ideal. It is the force of character proceeding
from a strong desire for realization which, by
giving their life a motive foreign to the preoccupation caused by their illness, endows them
with the power of resisting its debilitating in-
citements. This strength of character, however, should inspire in them an equal moder-
ation. It is never confined to obstinacy in the
connection that we have been speaking about.
There is more real energy in the application
of prudence than in that excess which is too
often due to ultra-nervousness. For the latter
strength is often indispensable. There are
miseries of a physiological nature which only an
operation can cure, but those of weak character
can not make up their minds to undergo one.
They postpone it, putting up with suffering that
poisons their life, and recoiling like cowards
from the necessary remedy. They thus drag out
a miserable existence, lacking the strength of
character which would free them from the suffering that they have not the strength to
struggle with successfully.

Does this mean that it behooves us to practise
the stoic doctrine in its pristine purity? Other
times other manners. We are too habituated

to a life of well-being to follow with ease the
example left us by the great dead.   But even if
we tried this, would we not be striking a note
in the harmonious ensemble that success demands.   In fine, it is important, above all, to
regard the stoic wisdom as the resultant of a
spirit of resignation not easily admitted by our
age.

Men of the present day should be combative;
it is from this point of view that it is essential
that they measure their strength with physical
pain, but by showing it they give proof of inferiority.   We are no longer annihilated by
society, but are become part of its active ma-
chinery.

Resignation, to be sure, is a very worthy
form of strength of character, but it must only
intervene after accomplishment.   It is only
when one is convinced of the futility of his acts
that he should resign himself to submit to what
it is beyond his power to avoid.   But up to the
moment when this has been proved one should
struggle by every means that strength of character suggests against the invasion of any evil
whose increasing would mean our diminution.

CHAPTER IV

OPPOSING THE ASSAULTS OF
DESTINY

EVERY human being is responsible for his
own development, is the architect of his own upbuilding. That is to say, it is the duty of each
one to make a thorough inquiry into the sentiments that master him, and he must rely upon
his strength of character to alter or modify
them in the way that seems most profitable for
his self-improvement. Various tendencies may
have upon determinations a directing influence
which will incline them to this side or that. It
is only by virtue of strength of character that
harmony will come to dominate. This faculty,
moreover, is susceptible of dissimilar applica-
tions according to the nature of the impressions
it brings out or suppresses. It supposes, then,
natural feelings as well as conditional or contrary feelings, according to the nature of that
which it is a question of encouraging or destroying.

What we call destiny is usually nothing more than the ensemble of facts provoked by our attitude toward events. To believe that destiny is something immovable, something inscribed, as it were, in the book of fate, would be to discourage all initiative, to fetter all perseverance. It would sanction moral and physical inertia and be an incitement to belief in fatalism. In fact, if one admits that it is impossible to struggle against destiny, what good are efforts aimed at bettering things? Why arm against a catastrophe that we can not avoid? Why not remain inert when it is useless to give battle, leaving destiny to work its will.

This is a doctrine cherished by the feeble because it gives them an excuse and a pretext. It is their excuse for inaction made to those to whom they must render an account. Also it is a pretext they love to give themselves for apathy. When through their negligence the thing that they have made a vague attempt at miscarries, they never fail to make some such remark as, "Well, what can we do? This thing was not to succeed." Or, "Fate is against me; one can not fight against destiny." It is such principles as these that swell the ranks of the incapable and the indolent. The fact is that one

II.4

must fight against destiny, and numbers of
people there are who know how to conquer it.
The hostile forces that so many persons pretend
environ them simply emanate from themselves
and their feebleness. They are the instincts that
will does not discipline and which lack the
favorable guidance of sane reason. What would
you think of him who instead of trying to build
up a fortune of his own, remained inactive with
the remark, ''When destiny wills it I shall become rich.'' The chances are that unless he is
provided for destiny will decline to interest itself in such a worthless individual, and will let
him die of hunger.

Destiny is ever blind and deaf, and we can
not make it hear or regard us. It is cruel and
unjust, and, as the saying is, knocks at random.
But are we certain that we have never deserved
its blows and done what is necessary to parry
them? There are people whose alleged misfortunes would constitute real happiness for
more sensible persons.

Every one has heard the story of the coach
that broke down. Its occupant took the road
for the nearest village where he inquired for
a vehicle, adding that he had been forced to
abandon his own because it was done for. There

was a man in the inn who overheard the
traveler; without saying a word he set out for
the scene of the accident, found the carriage, and
set to work fixing it. On the morrow he ap-
prized the traveler that in return for a sum
named he would engage to procure him a vehicle
that would take him to his destination. The
proposition was accepted and it was not without
a good deal of surprize that the traveler found
himself facing his own carriage which, by the
owner's too ready discouragement, had become
the property of the man who was able to put it
to some use.

We are apt too often to act like this traveler
when overtaken by an unforeseen misfortune.
We yield to barren discouragement, while another less weak would take advantage of this
event that we regard as a calamity, and lacking
complete success would extract a certain measure
of consolation from circumstances regarded by
us irreparable.

This furnishes an example of the trait of
strength of character of which we have just
been speaking, the trait which develops in us
the ability to combat that obscure entity which
the feeble call destiny and men of character
name the future.

One works out his own happiness, whatever pessimists may say. This faculty of enjoyment we carry within us, but with the feeble it remains in embryonic state, its power of expansion being limited to those imbued with sufficient strength of character to bring it to light.

Happiness is not what so many persons think it to be. The greater part of those who complain that they have never met with it represent it to themselves under the form of a sky that no cloud has ever darkened. These persons are ever ready to overwhelm with reproaches adverse fortune just as soon as the slightest thing happens to alter the inexact formula that represents it for them. Such people are like the Sybarite of antiquity who, finding nothing to reproach fate with, and *blasé* on all kinds of happiness, complained of being wounded by the petals of roses which strewed his couch.

No, happiness does not reside in a succession of great joys ending in enthusiasm. Considered thus, it becomes a Utopia, the impossibility of its realization being the punishment of those who have had the weakness to believe in it. Happiness is within us; it surrounds us; it lies in grateful harmony, in the comprehension of the things of nature; it is made of the admiration that we feel at the sight of a beautiful sunset, of the satisfaction we have in hearing a fine musical composition. In a more prosaic way we find it in family life, in the sweetness of friendship, in the pride of success achieved after long effort.

For certain of the elect it resides in the conception of personal value and in consciousness of progress toward self-perfection. For the savant it lies in discovery, and even in the researches that lead to the desired result. For all, in fine, it consists not in things of imposing character but in a series of humble satisfactions the sum of which is enough to counterbalance the inevitable boredom of existence.

We are here referring to habitual conditions only; we have not taken account of great catastrophes such as wreck lives, leaving nothing but débris after them. But even in the latter case it must not be forgotten that we can rebuild on the ruins; and indeed, for the most part, it is out of the crumbled material of demolition that new buildings are often constructed.

This is not addrest to persons of feeble character, who are prone to sit and weep amid ruins. Such as these are likely to go a long time without shelter. I am speaking to the strong, to those of virile character who will never admit defeat and lose no time in weeping; these have something better to do—to act; misfortune with them is belittled; soon it is forgotten; or eventually is transformed by them into prosperity. Even if circumstances do not permit them to reconstruct their initial success, they never consume themselves in foolish regrets, but make the best possible use of the new conditions. They will force themselves to forget the bad features of the situation, and extract from it only the good.

"I never knew the delights of walking," remarked a man of this sort of character, "until after I was ruined. Formerly I always used to ride, and never had a chance to enjoy the beauties of the road; now I go on foot, wondering at everything that I used hardly notice, and thankful for the misfortune that has given me so many little pleasures hitherto unsuspected."

Happiness, as conceived by a great many people, can not help becoming monotonous in time. Is not boredom well represented in a person having the means of instantly gratifying every possible desire? It is the delight of strong characters to conquer by a struggle the things

they covet. Having longed for them, they set
their whole will to obtaining them. How precious
now is their possession!

Such as these never became *blasé*, since the
bent of their character, whose strength incites
them to militant labor, always tends to the attainment of a new goal, the preceding one having
been reached. Those who know how to will and
act rarely become the playthings of destiny;
they have the world for a stage whereon to
exercise their faculties, and food for interest
is never lacking. With such persons resignation is not a habitual trait—far from it. Resignation accords little with force of character.
It is praiseworthy only as a transient virtue.
With strong men resignation is a sort of meditation; it is the homage that they render to the
violence of circumstances, the recognition of
their temporary supremacy. Now the very consciousness of a superior force proves strength of
judgment; it can not but produce desirable results, for it implies the resolution to adopt a
line of conduct which tho unadapted for the
time being will be profitable in the future, when
cool judgment and organized resistance can be
brought to bear. Only fools hurl themselves at
an impregnable wall. Those endowed with

strength of character measure with the eye the instruments needed to surmount the obstacle. The feeble, after a seeming attempt, allow themselves to sink to the ground in sterile resignation.

The word resignation is too often employed to designate the temporary acceptation of an inevitable misfortune. The strong are never willingly resigned, or at least their resignation is nothing more than an armistice during which they meditate their next attack. The apparent resignation of these is often merely the stoicism of which we have already spoken. Now we must not confound moral stoicism with stoicism in presence of physical ills. The latter is the very creditable opposing of one force to another force, against which indifference is the most potent weapon. The former consists of careful reflection with a view to attenuate the consequences, or to take measures against the act which seems about to overwhelm us. To this kind of courage is also given the name of philosophy; it is what permits us to endure adverse fortune and, at need, to return blow for blow.

Another form of strength of character is patience. This denotes under its silent aspect a kind of energy that is not appreciated as much

as it deserves to be. Patience has done more
for the happiness of many a destiny than have
qualities of the most brilliant type. To put it in
practise is needed more strength than is required
for action. Action tries the nerves, replies to
a need for exteriorization from whence always
results a certain solace. But that which is in
expectation demands a great deal of self-mastery
which strength of character alone can develop.
To take part with apparent impassibility in
great events effecting our interests is an effort
possible only to virile souls; and to accomplish
it with success the latter must be impregnated
with the qualities we have described.

There is still another kind of patience in the
arsenal of character which may be used against
the assaults of destiny. It is that which, born
of plodding perseverance, moves on obscurely
but surely toward its goal, destroys one after
another all obstacles, and arrives at the heart of
its objective before the enemy has divined its
presence. It is the virtue of those who undertake enterprises of great range; where nervousness or haste would compromise all, they wait
enduringly for the hour to show themselves and
then act in good earnest. Some will say, when
these succeed, that destiny has shown them par-

tiality. But would not it be more just to give
them credit for the strength of character they
have availed themselves of, and to cite them as
examples for the dull and impatient who, having
spoiled their work by inopportune hastiness
never fail to calumniate and complain of fortune's blows.

As a general principle, one should always mistrust those who complain of their lot. Destiny
is cruel only to the weak who do not know how
to resist its blows. It is merciful for men of
strong will who brave it face to face and compel
it to mercy by the power of character, engender-
ing by turn energetic resolves and patient man-
euvers, expectant action, and militant initiative; add to this a certain assumption of weakness—a formidable weapon, showing itself in
the guise of a temporary inertia suddenly transformed into deeds of courage and intelligence.

CHAPTER V

THE STRUGGLE AGAINST EN-
FEEBLING SENTIMENT

THE sentiment that strength of character has most frequent need of exerting itself against is love in all its forms. This sentiment, when conceived by strong natures and addrest to those worthy of comprehending it, can become an unrivaled comforter.

Maternal love in its highest expression is the lever that can remove numberless obstacles; it is also the *viaticum* that enables children to set out bravely upon life's journey. The love of parents for their children, accordingly as it is impregnated or not with the enlightened firmness that comes of strength of character, may be for them a safeguard or a baleful gift. Many parents imagine that they fail in their duty unless they show their children an indulgence which sometimes degenerates into culpable weakness. This kind of indulgence, it is well to realize, is rarely due to fine feeling. It generally answers to a narrow egotism, which yields

57

to the child the thing it desires when it would be wiser to refuse it. The most common cause of the spoiling of children, as it is called, is a certain thoughtless selfishness which makes the mother dread the little one's crying, as something disagreeable. She yields to the child on the plea of love and goodness, being unable to refuse it anything. How much more intelligent is the love of those parents who can resist a storm of tears and are able to make the child understand the reasons for refusing its wish. If the child is too young to reason with, the parent's strength of character will none the less make its influence felt and the baby mind will perceive the first gleam of the idea of duty. Later on, virile qualities will show themselves in such children and impel them in the right direction.

Another debilitating kind of sentimentality relates to the question of separation. Many parents prefer to see their children vegetate near them, rather than have the satisfaction of knowing that they are happy and prosperous at a distance. Such blind affection gives rise to sentiments that are most debilitating. Nothing encourages in children such mental flabbiness as the attempt to spare them all responsibility.

The strong men are those who could not be held
in the maternal nest after they had reached the
boundary of childhood, and whose parents had
admonished them early of life and its respon-
sibilities.

Does this mean that the children should quit
their parents and take flight like the birds of the
air as soon as their wings are fledged? Nothing
is farther from our desire than to do anything
to sap the wonderful institution of the family.
But in order that this institution should conserve all its value and attractiveness it should
always be a haven, never a prison. The home
loses its charms just as soon as these become
obligatory; constraint has never yet welded
souls; while a gentle firmness joined to an ample
range of ideas implying a wise freedom of conduct result in that mutual understanding without which any association based on affection
can not exist.

It is the same with friendship. This perfect
union of hearts and minds abhors affectation as
much as it does obstinacy. Friendship does not
mean an exclusive reciprocal sentiment. It consists in that fulness of devotion to which
strength of character sometimes gives the stamp
of sacrifice. Friendship is never perfect until

it is denuded of petty incidents which, far from
augmenting it, impart to it the character of a
selfish passion. When addrest to a person of the
weak type it can become positively atrophied,
with the result of producing a kind of moral
fragility; for if a strong soul is frequently seen
to communicate its virility, it is not a rare thing
to recognize degeneracy in him who binds himself by ties of friendship to one of feeble character whose inclinations he is powerless to guide.
Nothing is more contagious than softness and in-
consistency. This may be accepted as a rule
without exception. When two human beings
help each other by a mutual interchange of
moral qualities, the resulting friendship will
form their characters and make them blend.
The stronger intellectually must then make an
effort to fashion his friend in his own image;
if not, he will find himself becoming the reflection of the other.

There is another sentiment which, when
shared by noble minds, can become the ornament
of life. Love does not comport with ignoble
minds, for if it did it would straightway take
its place among the unavowable passions. It
must show itself, after a noble fashion, without
any hint of prudery, a thing which always de-

notes a subjection to sensual motives. · The giving of oneself should always be the seal of the union of two souls who are impelled toward moral beauty, encouraged by a certain loftiness of character which will preserve them from all · that soiling contact so menacing to the poorest ⌐ of sentiments.

To the married, strength of character is indispensable, since it enables them to tolerate · without bitterness each other's mutual frailties. · Perfection is not of this world, and it is difficult to exact it when one thinks how far he is from possessing it himself.

Patience, indulgence, of which we have just been speaking, are therefore virtues worth cultivating if we are to live a harmonious life.

There remain circumstances in which strength of character may intervene successfully. In the first place, we must give consideration to the impulses that a fleeting sentiment may set in motion. People of weak character yield readily to the solicitation of the moment. The flutter of sense is something they can not resist. They have not learned to make distinction between the race-instinct and the emotions whose principle rests in the attaining to a higher evolution. Character bulwarks the directing idea of all sentiment, striking its roots in aspirations which are beyond the reach of physiological considerations. Gross appetites are merely the portion of those whose brittleness of character makes it impossible for them to maintain themselves in the higher regions where self-mastery is supreme. By opposing our too-instinctive desires by strength of mind we can prevent their undue extension; especially can we effect this by trying to alter their course in making them blend in the noble enthusiasm of some great idea. This is the way to keep from pitfalls, which we look back upon with astonishment, so easily might they have been avoided.

It is profitable to associate this powerful sentiment with the diverse elements of personality as well as with the qualities of the object itself, to the end that we may blend what there is of instinct into a harmonious whole based on the sympathy of souls. The vertigoes, the excesses, the debasement caused by passional emotions illreprest may all be avoided by him who has made it a law always to oppose the impulse of nascent passion by the power of reason.

Fragile sentimentality has still another regrettable result, it tends to skepticism. Successive disillusions always engender a penchant for

doubt, that destroyer of self-confidence. Those
are rare in number who will confess that their
self-deceptions are due to the characteristic trait,
which is speedily determined by constant obedi-
ence to instinct. Instead of yielding to the
thorough self-examination of conscience, dictated by strength of character, they prefer to
indict the inconstancy of others, summing up in
their condemnation the whole sex whom they
hold responsible for their suffering. A serious
reliance upon themselves, through meditation,
would quickly show them the emptiness of their
recriminations. They would recognize that
their light-mindedness, their enslavement to
physical emotion, are the main causes of the dis-
enchantment which leaves them broken. They
will be convinced of the emptiness of ignoble
passion and will make the firm resolution never
again to engage the heart without the soul. Even
in this last case, however, it may be admitted
that sentimental error is not included and may
become the source of grievous suffering. But
those who have strong character will be enabled
to find in a diversion strongly willed, a means of
consolation for evils which in time will diminish
to the point that it will require an effort of
memory to resuscitate the old sorrow, now buried

under preoccupations calm and sane. They can thus congratulate themselves on having by manly effort escaped the thrall of debilitating sentiments, a sort of tyranny that reason and conscience alike disallow.

There are still other passions which, if not restrained by firmness of mind, take the shape of an invading host, marring and usurping the realm of character and preventing its development. They begin, for the most part, by tendencies that thrive on moral atony, becoming in time dangerous. It is soon time to tear them up by the roots, but indolence does not permit the necessary effort and we quietly allow them to grow into defects of which we become the slaves. It has now become impossible to escape their exigencies. Self-mastery neglected revenges itself, and the vassalage of ignoble ideas asserts its rule over the non-resistant. In each individual there are a number of "egos" which often find themselves in opposition. Now for insufficiently nourished souls nothing is more weakening than internal conflict. What must be done is to supplant one desire by another, one appetite by another appetite.

What means has any one of seeing clearly into himself unless strength of character supervenes

to impose its logic and direction? Those who do
not know how to summon their aids in the hour
of trouble are like the bird that dashes himself
against the wires of his cage, seeking an outlet
that does not exist till some one opens the door.

Strength of character is the bay opening upon
the seas of moral liberty—and material liberty
too, we may add—for mastery of self engenders
success whence flows independence. Mental
strength, then, not only is the cause of moral
liberty but is also a means of acquiring individual liberty.

Perhaps we have already used up too much
ink in establishing the parallel between individual restraint and social restraint to linger
any longer upon the subject. None the less we
must insist upon this point; moral liberty engenders individual liberty whence proceeds, in a
certain measure, social liberty. We say in a
certain measure, for no civilized human being
can disengage himself from his duties to his kind.
These obligations, however, may be agreeable
and comforting, provided that they are per-
formed freely and by personal choice. Binding
in their nature, they should rarely be of the instinctive sort.

All designs looking to the betterment of others

should be guided by reason. To act without consulting it would mean yielding to acts of impulse, especially to egotism, which, in the absence of reflection, dictates all human actions. This would be to bring upon the scene vanity and stupidity, whose consequences go on multiplying by the piling up of the errors they involve. Goodness without strength of character is a feeble virtue, working at random and at the hazard of momentary fancy. Those, moreover, who practise it, if they are honest, admit to themselves the inferiority of their motives. Unreasonable goodness is often nothing more than sensibility based on egotism. We relieve another's suffering so that he will stop bothering us, altho our motive never appears to us in the brutal form in which we here depict it. There are, in fact, very few persons capable of thus analyzing their intentions. It is apparent in this connection that, if the suffering were felt by some unknown person, and did not touch us, we would be in no hurry to go to the rescue.

There is in small charitable manifestations an unconscious egotism which we translate by pity, a sentiment that comes of our satisfaction at having escaped the suffering we relieve. The goodness which is tempered by strength of character knows nothing of these transactions, ignored by ourselves but thoroughly debilitating in their effect. It acts without evoking the personal element to the slightest extent. It will sometimes take on the aspect of insensibility, but the feelings it elicits are always of lasting quality, and its motives, being of the higher order, give to its realizations a largeness of range unknown to the common type of goodness, which acts without knowing whither it tends or what may be its results.

Pity, when it does not possess equality and aim at rehabilitation, may also be classed among the debilitating sentiments. It may be acquired by the cultivation of reason. The idea of protection, unless it involves aspiration toward equality, always has a lessening effect upon its object. Sentimentality is the last consideration for him who wishes to take character for his guide. Does this mean that he must be hard-hearted and without feeling? The best way to answer this question is by asking another. Are those who make a display of sentiment, themselves exempt from selfishness? And since this is the trait that is the most common, and that which stamps nearly all, why not make of it a source of strength instead of allowing ourselves to be shackled by it? Why not transform an obstacle into a weapon of defense?

Reasonable egoism may be more fruitful of pity, when freely avowed and directed toward a noble object, than when it is disguised in the traits of banal goodness, whose manifestations, always ephemeral and insufficient, belittle the one to whom they are addrest in emphasizing his inferiority and dependence.

CHAPTER VI

FEAR, AND STRENGTH OF CHARACTER

ONE can not help pitying, while also slightly despising, those whom lack of will-power renders slaves to that tormenting weakness, fear.

Fear is a kind of shadow constantly hovering over life, for it has no need of reason for its existence. It shows itself in everything, poisoning moments the most delightful, spoiling the most legitimate pleasures. Fear is a sort of anguish caused by a danger, real or imaginary, and seems to involve powerlessness to will anything except retreat. Usually it has no reason for its existence, since it is far from furnishing a solution of any kind. True, in most cases, the object of terror being undefined, retreat is an instinctive resort; it means escaping some unknown danger, the presence of which nothing suggests. At times fear is of partly unconscious nature, participating in the instinct of conservation. The sensitive feel it at the slightest approach of danger. It is almost impossible to conquer it without having resort to strength of character, for reasoning has no effect upon persons prone to fear.

Every one tries to convince nervous people of the harmlessness of thunder. Nearly every one knows that the danger is past when the clap of thunder is heard. Nevertheless, in spite of all scientific proof, in spite of their own inward conviction, they tremble with apprehension after the flash of lightning, holding their ears in the most childish fashion.

Others have an invincible fear of darkness. They know perfectly well there is nothing in the darkness, but they would not venture into it for the whole world. For them deprivation of light constitutes actual suffering; they people the obscurity with a fantastic world of menacing larvæ and fantoms.

Those who are afflicted with this weakness can not cultivate too earnestly strength of character, which will give them prohibition against a return of their agonizing terrors.

For their fear is caused by nothing else than weakness. This is the necessary deduction of all who have ever been among the timorous. The slightest company, no matter if it be some one weaker than themselves, reassures them.

They do not reflect that in case of attack their companion will be more embarrassment than aid; for the proper trait of fear is not to reflect at all. If persons given to fear took the trouble to think, they would perceive that their defect has a contemptible foundation; mistrust of their own merits and an exaggerated idea of weakness, which can be reassured by the presence of a child. If they kept their ideas clear they would see that such company, instead of an advantage, would be an additional reason for disquiet. For if there were any real danger, it would be their duty to protect the child, who would thus add to the complications. We do not admit that they might think of abandoning it, but if such an idea should occur to them it would furnish one example the more to show to what lengths fear will go in annihilating all moral sense. Their painful anxiety over, and sane reason reinstated, they are likely to blush at themselves for their conduct, and this will be a step in the right direction.

Numbers of people imagine they exculpate themselves by the excuse, "I lost my head for the moment." This excuse aggravates the matter, for to lose one's head is the most blamable of all weaknesses. One could hardly pardon a child for resorting to this pretext, but in an adult it is the *cachet* of impotence as well as the confession of defeat.

Fear, like many maladies, is particularly contagious; it is communicated to children in stories told by nurses who, especially if unenlightened, risk poisoning the lives of their charges and those belonging to them. For cowards like to make converts; it seems that their defect takes on a less shameful aspect the more it is diffused, and they love to spread the contagion among those that surround them.

For this weakness there is only one remedy—strength of character, which will maintain the will-power sufficient for the struggle. It is usually more than useless to reason with the timorous, especially at the critical moment, their reply to all arguments being, "I am afraid." The simplest way is not to try to convince them they are wrong in yielding to fear, but to supply them with the means of mastering their weakness. One way is to send the timid one into a darkened room for something, having convinced him that there is nothing there to fear. Only on his return should recourse be had to the language of reason. Let the first attempt at treatment be simply an order.

The timid are nearly always obedient; their nature leaves them open to impression by a superior will, and fear of the complications involved in rebellion induces them to overcome their defect. The first victory ought immediately to be followed up by a second one. To accustom the patient to darkness should be one of the first cares in the reforming of a timid nature. He should be accompanied at first and got used to it, and the conversation should avoid all disquieting subjects.

It is to be noted, further, that those given to cowardice are prone to recall those things that frighten them. With teeth chattering they will talk of ghosts and apparitions, and it is difficult to awaken in their minds the recollection of subjects other than terrifying. Setting apart this unhealthy propensity to seek after sensations of fanciful nature, which recall certain maniacs who take pleasure in aggravating a wound, this habit must be ascribed to the unique preoccupation that haunts their brain in the darkness. This is why it is necessary to give their thoughts a different direction. And, later on, when they are sent into the dark alone for a few minutes, care must be taken to demand of them something requiring them to reflect a little before answering, the response to be deferred till their return from their little adventure.

Fear does not resist the power of derogatory thoughts, and he who can conquer sufficient strength of character to bring about this resistance is very near to a victory over this hideous defect which is so fatal to the sufferer.

Still another source of fear that moral strength may come to sap to some extent is the tendency to superstitious beliefs, which deform the mind by substituting for judgment some absurd belief repulsive to reason. There exist perfect skeptics in religious matters who turn pale as they see a crow flying on their left. Others will never undertake anything on Friday. Still others there are who would not for the whole world take a decisive step on Friday, should it fall on the thirteenth of the month. Certain men, otherwise intelligent, fill their lives with these superstitions, with the result that their intellectual faculties become tainted. It is only by force of character that they can free themselves from such enslavement.

These, just like the victims of fear, should study the sources of their beliefs, and honestly acknowledge that they are based solely on traditions established by coincidences. Legends of apparitions are nothing but the result of unnatural observations. Superstitions relating to such or such encounters, or to some incident or other, are the result of some remark lightly, or perhaps designedly, made. There are none so blind as those who will not see, as the saying is; and we may add there is no worse clairvoyant than he who is bent on seeing some particular thing. Now, one imbued with a superstitious mind finds coincidents in the most ordinary circumstances. Let some pleasure come to him when he happens to be wearing a certain costume, and he will put it on again in the hope that his walk will bring the desired result. If, on the contrary, on meeting some person bad luck follows, he will try to avoid him for the future or examine into every thing that happened on the day of the meeting.

Superstition is always based upon superficial observation, and denotes feebleness of mind which should be combated by reason. To impose resistance of any value upon excessive credulity character must intervene. We must oblige ourselves to act as if we were untouched by superstition. Just as soon as it points to some act which must be avoided, that is the very thing to do, if it is not something wrong. On the other hand, we must be on our guard against what the arbitrary creed prescribes. For example, some one upsets the salt cellar; instead of being in a hurry to throw salt over the left shoulder (interrupting the conversation the while), lest bad luck should fall on the company, use some will-power, refrain from flinging salt over your shoulder, and take up the conversation at the point where it was halted by the accident. Then in all honesty ask yourself conscientiously what are the consequences of this abstention. When it is established that no misfortune has happened as a result of disregarding the prescribed exorcisms the inanity of the popular belief will be admitted. No real relationship being seen to exist, reason will oppose itself to a number of similar unexpected happenings. But before we can invoke reason it is urgent that we resolve to follow the counsels which flow from deductions made in cold blood and devoid of partiality.

Character, then, is indispensable in inspiring the courage essential for sane reasoning, and also for keeping the resolutions prompted by such reasoning. In the cure of fear it will intervene in the way we have described; and from the time that improvement is observable the patient should try to continue himself his education in courage.

The means most certain and that we can not insist enough upon is to substitute for thoughts of fearful nature those totally different, yet in-. teresting enough to make an impression upon the mind, but detrimental to what it is desired to do away with. No one has ever been mastered by a violent sentiment without perceiving that the ordinary fears that assail him instantly vanish. We often hear of cowards who become paralyzed with fear in the dark, setting out int the middle of the night for a doctor without feeling any of the terrifying sensations that ordinarily assail them. The reason is that their brain, dominated by the thought of the help that must be got, the preoccupation of haste and the worry caused by the illness of some dear one, has room for no idea except the agonizing one of the moment. In presence of that all others vanish. The immediate representation does away with all others, and fear flies before an emotion stronger still.

To conquer fear, then, it suffices to have recourse to the things that contribute to make strength of character; the will to possess them. This may pass for a jest with some. They will

say that if you need will in order to get possession of it "the fat's in the fire," for they acknowledge themselves to be incapable of shaping
any .desire with intensity.

The thing to do is not to try to conquer will-
power at the first blow; it is enough to have
some valid hope of success in this direction.

This is the first step. The second consists in
strengthening oneself for the attempt, and not
offering any resistance to the doctrine itself.

To recognize one's weakness and have the
desire for deliverance is the chief condition
demanded for the development of a firm character. Meanwhile we must force ourselves to
abandon all superstition and enfranchise ourselves from fear, just as we would divest ourselves of some uncomfortable, worn-out garment.

We have no time for the weaknesses of former
epochs. We of the present age must all struggle
with more or less ardor and also earnestness
to conquer the place we covet and which often
belongs to us by right. The coward is often,
vis-à-vis of his adversaries, in the situation of a
man disarmed and wishing to measure himself
against an enemy equipped with shield and
dagger. Against such a foe one weapon only
is possible—strength of character, which permits

its possessor to think, to resolve, and to act.
He who has this and can adapt it to circumstances may face every hostile front. He is
certain to issue from the fight victorious and
regenerated.

PART II

CHARACTER: HOW TO DE-
VELOP IT FOR BUSI-
NESS AND DAILY
LIFE

CHAPTER I

EXERCISES OF THE INTELLECT FOR ACQUIRING STRENGTH OF CHARACTER

ADMITTING that a little will-power is necessary in order to act upon the will, he who suffers from weakness of character and desires to fortify his mind should allow this comparison to sink deep in his memory:

A gardener desiring to cultivate certain plants of precious kind, begins, before sowing the seed, by freeing the soil from the tares which are fatal to growth. As soon as the seeds have sprouted he further relieves them of all dangerous environment by tearing away all parasite growths, which, in spite of his care, continue to show themselves and quickly hinder the blooming of the flowers, those objects of his solicitude. These freed from their invading foes are not slow to spring up and spread their leaves, choking in turn the thin grass which grows poorly in their shade.

He who wishes to obtain strength of char-

acter should, then, above all else, try to deliver
his mind from the invasion of feeble thoughts.
Before seeking strength he should expel every
idea of weakness; this is what might be called
clearing the soil. It also gives a valid answer
to those who pretend that fragile wills can never
be improved, since, in order to arrive at strength
of character, that qualification itself is essential.

In order to will to advantage it is necessary
above all to do away with the enemies of volition.
Now all weakness willed is a primordial obstacle
to the installation of strength of character. For
one who aspires to will-power, therefore, it is
essential to avoid the thoughts opposed to its
manifestations.

Resistance to willing is itself a form of willing; those, therefore, who say they are too indolent to guide their desires in the direction of
strength unconsciously perform an act of the
will. Would it not be more worth while if this
contrary force were employed in the acquisition
of so essential a quality, rather than utilized
against its possession? It is certain that the act
of developing moral vigor sufficient to impart
energetic direction demands qualities of a special
order and a regimen that can not be acquired
over night. But before *willing much* it is always

possible to try *to will a little*. The conquest of
strength of character often rises out of the
débris of moral inaction, and the latter disap-
pears just as soon as the power of volition
begins to take form in the mind which has
rid itself of weakness and its depressing cortège.

The first condition, then, of this evolution is
an aspiration toward the mastering of oneself, and it is not without a certain amount of
agitation that this desire takes shape. It is
even desirable that this emotion should take
place, since from the antagonism between the
old and the desired state arises nearly always a
resolution that may be regarded as the embryo
of character.

It has often been said by the wise that the
finest victory that a man can put to his credit
is that which he has gained over himself.

His resolution taken, he should enter upon
the struggle against excessive emotions. Having
estimated their value as the result of the first
·impression he will make certain to attribute to
them their exact significance. He will on no
account delay very long over the primitive sen-
sation. As soon as possible after the initial
shock he will impose upon himself a certain
moral coldness, that is to say, he will avoid

giving his imagination free rein for comment
and deduction. It may even be prudent to call
in some idea foreign to the incident in question.
All this has no other aim than the settling down
of the effervescence caused by the emotion, and
always perilous for the thought.

People have a sorry habit of studying consequences in a disfiguring light. Amplification
does the rest, and we soon find ourselves upon
the threshold of resolves which, considered in
the light of the event which prompted them, become perfectly unreasonable. For example, a
person of weak character hears of a relative's
illness. It is a question of a widow left with a
little daughter. Straightway moral debility
begins its work. The person becomes excited by
the usual anticipations of pessimistic natures. On
receiving the news she imagines they have not
told her the truth, that the relative is going to
die, and the child be left in her charge. The
cortège of worries and privations that will result
from this augmenting of her family defiles before her imagination, and, frightened by the
thought of the responsibility about to fall upon
her, she loses her head, forms resolutions which
she directly abandons for new ones, and ends
by making a mess of it all.

On the morrow she learns that her relative
is better, and her high spirits make her forget
all her anxiety on the sick woman's account, her
imagination having cured the patient just as it
had killed her.

If she had chosen to acquire some strength
of character she might have acted differently.
On receiving the bad news she should have
represt all thoughts tending to make things
worse, and waited for more information before
making a decision.

But that is impossible, you will say, since such
efforts are beyond reach of weak characters.
The fact is that we do not require it of them at
the very first.

When a person who has not yet achieved the
conquest of himself finds himself face to face
with some event designed for his overthrow his
sole effort should be brought to bear upon one
thing: to concentrate his ideas instead of dis-
sipating them.

To do this he should be content with register-
ing the fact, and then he should *immediately
occupy himself with something else* for fifteen
minutes up to an hour.   To anticipate objection
to the impossibility of this, we offer advice that
will be continued at some length.

For example, one may write one or two letters in advance; this is an easy diversion. It is understood that in the letters there need be no question of what we have just learned, and the more the object of our preoccupation haunts the mind the more must we contrive to banish it. Write, then, without mentioning it, as if the letter has got the start of it by an hour. We are then rid of it for the time being, and if it is something that must be communicated to our correspondent it may be imparted when the moment of excitement is past.

The object of this exercise is to collect our ideas and prevent representations from crowding in disorder in an overtaxed brain. This accomplished, and the letter or letters written, emotion will be felt to subside, and we shall be able to think to some purpose. If, however, the thought brought back to the object that caused the agitation will not attain to coordination, if one feels himself carried away by a flood of apprehensions it will be necessary to reject them all before they become preponderant, employing meanwhile the prescribed means up to the moment when it is given to us to consider dispassionately the consequences of the thing that is tormenting us.

When we have attained to silence, and only then, we shall begin to reflect. Above all it is essential to force ourselves to take an optimistic course. It is the defect of the inconsistent to see everything in dark colors. Strong souls, on the contrary, try to search out even in shameful incidents, the features that are least so, in order to supply the more easily the remedy. It is, then, necessary to view things on their least painful side, while avoiding at the same time the lure of chimerical hope—for deceptions are bad counsellors to strength. If there be question of those things that carry in their train inevitable consequences we must face them without hesitation. To palliate them or refuse to see them as they are would be weakness. It is hard to walk in the dark, and to avoid ambushes it is well to light up the road. The thing of primary importance is to mistrust the first impulse and avoid the initial period of mental confusion. This achieved, one shall have taken a long step in the acquisition of strength of character.

A vice which is common in all those of weak character is anger. This they allow full headway because of a momentary sense of solace that it procures for them.

Passion is never the trait of virile natures.

They know what inferiority is stamped upon those afflicted by this habit, and they try with all the power of their will not to give way to it.

Anger is not always spontaneous with the weak. It is often the resultant of the accumulation of the representations of which we were speaking a moment ago. In common parlance, anger is said to mount, and the image is a correct one, for it is only by degrees, in certain cases, that anger invades the brain. The point of departure is often nothing more than some disagreement; but a strong imagination creates motives which give rise to irritation, which in turn increases in proportion as it registers them.

We may compare this kind of anger to a fire, harmless at first; but, built up and fed with care, it becomes a conflagration.

Passion, on the contrary, is produced suddenly and is appeased as soon as the image which has caused it no longer presents itself in vivid form. In feeble minds this attenuation occurs rapidly. They are incapable of keeping the same thought intact very long, so that the object of their resentment in passing through many rapid gradations is at last effaced.

This emotion takes on a progression directly

opposite to that of the other kind. While with these latter it follows an ascending gamut and for a long time maintains itself at its maximum intensity by the renewing of its motive forces, in the case of those carried away by passion there is a constant depression whose final phase is marked by an abatement as pronounced as is the agitation itself. In both cases the irritable are victims of this defect. Judgment obscured by passion supplies them with no sensible suggestions, and they have to regret all the resolutions they have made under the influence of this kind of emotion. Nothing but an energetic appeal to character can save them.

No one need laugh at the proverb which says: "When anger is in the ascendant roll the tongue seven times in the mouth before speaking." Put in this way, the advice may seem curious; none the less it contains profound wisdom. All who are seriously desirous to oppose their natural impatience by strength of character should ponder it and put it in practise, in spirit if not literally. `Let the aspirant for firmness of character, upon the appearance of irritation, impose upon himself some act that will divert his attention from the annoyance in question.

A German philosopher cites the case of a

man who was noticed carrying a chain which
from time to time he unrolled and manipulated
in silence. One day some one asked him the
reason of this. "This chain," he replied
smiling, "is my bridle. I am of a very irritable
temperament, and anger has often made me do
foolish things which I have deeply regretted.
So that I have made it a rule never to obey any
emotional impulse without first letting a few
moments elapse. As soon as any irritating incident rouses in me the spirit of retort, of too
ready desires or resolves, I deliberately count
the one hundred links of my chain, thus imposing on my mind a tension wholly bent in
making no mistake in my count. This to me is
an invaluable diversion. During the operation
my nerves calm down, the inward disturbance
is appeased, and in the mirror of my mind, now
clear, wise resolutions are peacefully reflected."

The philosopher has not told us any more;
but we like to think that after a while the bridle
was discarded and that he who conquered
strength of character by such original means did
not need to have recourse to it very long.

This example ought to be a lesson to all who
wish to make a conquest of character. We
have said before that it is wholly made up of

calmness and recollection, and without being obliged to employ such an eccentric process as that just cited, it is within the power of all to have recourse to some task at the moment when excitement is at its height. And this task, which need not interfere with the ordinary course of things, may just as well be of the moral as of the material order.

For instance, no one will notice it if a person takes out his pocket-book and counts over nine or ten cards put there expressly. The act will always be excused on the ground of forgetfulness, or of some possible error that it is necessary to guard against.

Other actions seemingly as natural as this may be arranged in advance.

During the moment we are employed in executing them the thought, forcibly diverted from its course by the act that we are engaged in and the slight effort of calculation it involves, will no longer present itself under the brutal aspect that anger clothed it with; and little by little, strength of character helping, actions of an outward character will no longer be indispensable. We shall gradually find it desirable to give our thoughts the character of contemplation, and the wished-for calm will soon come.

It would be an error to suppose that weakness can be got rid of so easily.

Relapses are sometimes numerous, but if one be strong in resolution he will remark that even relapses are the stepping-stones to firmness of character. The qualities of which this is composed are the progeny of reason. They are acquired by education and belong, like so many others, to the sphere of the practical.

Thanks to a methodical plan of vigorous elaboration and properly sustained after the manner indicated, we can bring about a sure calm after a period of agitation. The conditions of this superior evolution rest upon an initiative which can be sustained by strength of character alone. It is by this trait alone that we can know the serenity which is engendered by order and unity of thought, those elements that determine unity of action which is inseparable from success.

CHAPTER II

PHYSICAL EXERCISES FOR DEVELOP-
ING STRENGTH OF CHARACTER

IF the postulant follows conscientiously the
counsels that we have given in the preceding
chapter he will find himself disposed to wage
war to some advantage upon his own weaknesses, but this will not suffice to preserve him
from relapses and confirm him in sane and
reasonable volition. In order that these last
conditions may be fulfilled the forces of his
moral nature must be based upon the power that
may be obtained from physical exercises.

The first thing to do is to get rid definitely
of all impulsiveness; for this defect always degenerates into nervousness and then everything
must be begun over again. In the battle that
the weak must fight with themselves, nervousness is the most redoubtable foe, since it is an
element of disorganization. A moment's nervousness may destroy the fruits of the application of days. It fetters all reflection com-
prising a judgment and does not even leave will-

power for discussion. It bears about with it its pitiable excuse, the excuse of a man of brittle character put forth as an extenuating circumstance: "What can you expect, I was nervous at the time." Or the still more current one, "I had to relieve my nerves." It would be impossible to enumerate all the foolish actions to which these two terms have given illusory protection.

It is always best to proclaim aloud that this excuse is nothing but an aggravation of the fault it seeks to palliate. Commission of it is reprehensible, but to seek to explain it by nervousness is to have it thrown out of court. If the fault is a defect the sentiment that gave rise to its commission is another, and a more important one. He who invokes this pitiful defense is like one who would say: "I have done wrong because I am bad." It is then necessary at any cost to put a halter on impulsiveness and nervousness whenever they appear.

In connection with the exercises that we have just advised and which are related to the reflective faculty, we would also suggest exercises of physical character, with a view of conquering that kind of strength of character that we name endurance.

Endurance which takes root in moral volition demands, moreover, a certain quantity of physical energy to be maintained with success. It is the foundation stone of the edifice of character. Endurance is composed of a variety of sentiments that we shall briefly analyze:

Calmness.

A certain contempt for pain.

Patience.

Perseverance.

In the beginning of this book we stated what were the benefits to be derived from calmness. We will not return to the subject; but we are going to determine the physical means of obtaining it, having already in the preceding chapter pointed out how to conquer it in a moral sense.

Calmness is the state attained to by a man in whom moral and physical equilibrium is complete. It is a priceless possession from the fact that there are few moments in our day when it is not in requisition. The slightest incidents as well as the gravest events can cause us considerable inconveniences unless we encourage them with calmness of mind. But to be successful in the effort to keep a firm balance when subjected to the agitation of some emotion we must, as an indispensable condition, have recourse to certain physical aids. The mind can not attain to real courage unless the body comes to its aid, at least during the time of novitiate.

Having called calmness to our aid by the means that we prescribed in Part I of the book, and having, after the daily examination of conscience, slept the sleep that comes of a will at perfect peace, it will be well to revive the above thought and saturate ourselves with its meaning, previous to entering upon the exercises which follow:

FIRST EXERCISE

Take a piece of cardboard the size of a large sheet of paper. Cut a hole in this cardboard which will correspond in size to an ink-stain made on a piece of paper which is to be pasted to the wall.

While comfortably seated before the ink-stain take the cardboard by the lower rim between the thumb and index finger, the arm being extended well out from the body. Your care must now be to do what follows: Look through the hole of the cardboard at the ink-stain on the paper so that the stain is exactly enclosed, nothing of the white surface appearing to the eye.

For the first few days this visual and physical tension should not exceed twenty seconds; little by little the time may be extended. But the point is to be very particular about exactness in the experiment; no speck of white must appear to the eye during the test.

SECOND EXERCISE

We are to proceed in this as in the first, but in place of a piece of cardboard take a sheet of paper, and try to make the aperture frame the ink-stain for the eye while the paper keeps its stiffness. If the paper bends, the experiment must be tried again.

THIRD EXERCISE

Fill a glass with water to a third of an inch of the brim, and hold it toward the bottom. Hold it so that it will be on a level with a line traced on the wall.

The surface of the water in the glass must be held so that its level will not deviate from the line.

Hold the glass at arm's length from the body until you begin to feel fatigue.

When this exercise is kept up for a while it will be possible to do it without the slightest stirring of the water.

FOURTH EXERCISE

Fill the glass now to the very top and repeat the experiment.

If the water overflows, try again.

FIFTH EXERCISE

Having filled the glass to the brim, hold it up from the bottom by the thumb and fourth finger for two seconds; then move it slowly from right to left keeping its brim level with the line which it must just graze.

These exercises, which may have the look of being devised to provoke impatience, are not always crowned with success at the first attempt. And for this very reason those who apply themselves to them conscientiously and intelligently are in a fair way to conquer their nervousness, since in the course of their experiments they will have frequent occasion to fight against this defect.

Contempt for pain is in proportion to the appraisal of the pain or the importance with which imagination invests it. Is it necessary here to repeat the story of the sick man who felt himself cured while he was knocking at the physician's door?

It is an incontestable fact that pain is increased by the anxiety it provokes. Moreover, it exists in reality in most cases; but while those who cultivate strength of character lessen the force of pain by the contemptuous fashion in which they regard it, people of feeble will-power permit it such a preponderant place in their thoughts that it is impossible for them to forget it even momentarily.

Let us add that their natural wilfulness prevents them from taking up the hygienic exercises recommended by physical culture, and known to be a sovereign remedy for the physiological miseries which sap intellectual strength.

We shall not attempt a description of those exercises whose range exceeds the limits of our book, but in a general way we may suggest the possibility of getting control over their nerves, up to the point of being able to ignore habitual sufferings on a small scale by recourse to the following exercises:

First Exercise

In case of indisposition, headache, rheumatism, neuralgia, if the suffering is not too acute, one should resort to some diversion of intellectual nature. For instance, take up a book and read a page or two with the object of discovering some quality or some defect. Suppose goodness is the quality we fix upon, try then to find it manifested in the pages before us. Perhaps it may happen the book contains nothing but reasoning and that goodness does not figure there at all. None the less it will be noticed that the mind-tension involved in this reading directed to an object has altered the course of the suffering and deprived it of its intensity.

Second Exercise

The reading concluded, write down the gist of it and then develop it in a couple of pages.

Third Exercise

Reduce these two pages to ten lines while taking special care to condense the meat of the argument.

FOURTH EXERCISE

Then make the endeavor to reduce these ten lines to a phrase which will sum up all the observations contained in the passage.

This is addrest as much to those who are not given to intellectual occupations as to those habitually so engaged.

Apart from immediate and pressing interest the business in hand seldom has any power of distracting us from physical suffering; while the exercises we offer have a certain novelty and attractiveness which give them a better chance of success.

Under pretext of suffering we always feel an inclination to throw up our daily labor; but if we consider work from a higher point of view and something of the utmost importance there will remain no pretext whatever for neglecting it.

Patience may be obtained by putting it to the proof in the following way:

FIRST EXERCISE

Take a handful of lead ground up like grain; spread it out upon a white sheet of paper and count the grains four times in succession. If

after the first attempt there is the slightest sign
of impatience, the grains must be shuffled up
and the count recommenced. If the same number is not obtained at each count, try it over
until the identical number occurs three times
in succession.

SECOND EXERCISE

Attach a watch to the wall and without moving
a muscle watch the hands for a fixt time.

(At the beginning a few seconds will be sufficient.)

THIRD EXERCISE

Having preceded as prescribed above, perform certain identical motions for a fixt time.

For example, bring the thumbs together at
regular intervals, for a few seconds at first.

Then do the same with the index fingers and
the remaining fingers in turn.

The duration of these exercises should be increased a little each day and kept up until the
slightest sign of impatience has disappeared.

Perseverance can be acquired in the same
way. And in order to give the exercises some
useful aim it will be well to have some good
purpose in view, such as the rendering of some

service, etc. But the most important consideration of all is the determination to continue the exercises. For it must not be supposed that the mastery of ourselves is to be gained in a day. It is only to be conquered by force of will and perseverance. And this last quality will find very strong encouragement from the progress that will be observed to follow upon conscientious application. The results obtained will be a valuable aid in the achievement of our favorite ambitions.

After some days of these continued daily exercises the happy assurance will be had that nervous symptoms are becoming rarer. Physical ailing will be lessened, and we shall find ourselves giving it only the amount of attention it deserves and guarding against its encroachments. What would have passed for a catastrophe a few weeks ago is now reasonably set down for a very remediable evil. Pride of self-domination will be augmented by desire for self-perfection and the satisfaction of feeling immune from all dependence on the emotions will become the most active factor in the acquisition of that strength of character in whose practise are found consolement and encouragement.

CHAPTER III

STRENGTH OF CHARACTER IN BUSINESS

It is in truth the philosophy of another age than ours that inculcates contempt of riches.

It need not be taken for granted that we are going to make an apology for cupidity, yet we venture to assert that at the present time every one might profit by letting the thought of the great Schopenhauer sink into his mind:

"Money is a barrier against all possible evils."

Ignoring the arguments of puritans we shall explain and make some comment upon this thought of the great philosopher.

He did not say: money is the universal remedy; he denominated it a barrier.

And how exact this attribute is. Money prevents the sufferings that come of poverty. With money, we may ignore cold and hunger; while sickness can not be obviated by money, it can be considerably relieved by it. Money gives us the satisfaction of relieving others from suffer-

106

ing. By money one may aid in the development of nascent genius, participate in some fine achievement. It gives one the leisure to devote a part of his time to the culture of art under all its forms.

Add to this that money can provide a powerful diversion for all troubles, by permitting of distraction for the mind from the anxieties that assail it.

We are aware that pessimists will not omit to confront this argument with the famous line:

"And he who keeps guard at barriers of the Louvre can not protect our kings."

But at the risk of displeasing some we venture to say that it is less painful to die in a palace, surrounded by every possible comfort, than to end one's days on a pallet, where the lack of every comfort tends to increase the rigors of the last agony. With the tender care of the best physician attainable there is much less chance of our quitting this life than would be the case if we had to forego all this for lack of money. If money does not bring positive cure it always brings alleviation.

There is, then, no discussion of the subject possible. At the period we have reached it is

a bad thing to be poor; and we must try to get
a thorough understanding of all that we may
possibly do in an honorable and legitimate way
to remedy this condition of things if it exists;
or, if we belong among the privileged ones who
inherit wealth, we should take every means to
conserve it.

Now, the conditions of life ever becoming
more and more onerous, permit scarcely any one
to remain inactive. Even to those who have
received wealth as an inheritance idleness is a
certain cause of ruin. A great fortune exacts
genuine labor as a condition for efficiency of
administration. And those who leave to
strangers this duty do not long deserve the title
of millionaire; they soon see themselves reduced
to a simple competence which for their children
comes to be want. These shirkers, unless they
happen to have one of those rare birds, an
honest manager, pay the penalty of their negligence. The individual interests of the manager
always prevail over those of the master and
even abstracting the factor of indelicacy from
the situation, one can hardly require a man to
consider the interests of his employer above his
own.

This is why a rich man who wants to preserve

his fortune and even increase it ought first of all to be his own business manager.

Business is the point of departure and the chief aim of every one in the world, not excepting those placed at the head of the State; since in conducting the affairs of State these latter must also occupy themselves with their own. We will not even except artists who, provided they know how to draw from their works the price they are worth, can the more easily devote to their beloved ideals the time that their happy transactions places at their disposal.

What masterpiece can be expected of him who works for so much a day for his daily expenses. The finest talent is put in the same class with a trade and must be exercised without respite. In these conditions the finest dispositions are spoiled, the soaring thought, represt by manipulation, breaks before it can realize its fine aspirations, and is caught in a rut where it remains kept down forever.

An artist whom certain purists reproached for making a traffic of his genius made answer, "It is necessary for me to be a tradesman in order to have the right to be a genius." And history is full of facts which confirm his dictum. Are we not assured that Solon the sage paid the expenses of his trip to Egypt by selling oil and thus traveling in comfort? Or, coming nearer home, did not the great Shakespeare adopt the occupation of theatre-manager to obtain the necessary leisure to produce his dramatic masterpieces?

Business, therefore, under the multiple forms it takes is the labor intended for all. From the bottom to the top of the ladder it is necessary to amass money to apply it to some cause or other.

Money is not what the shiftless are tempted to regard it—something that exempts us from duty; it is, on the contrary, the means by which we may fulfil them in a larger, better way. Every one, then, should in his own way and at a certain time make an effort to amass some money.

Some there are who apply money to their daily wants. Others seek it to swell the fortune they desire to leave to their children. Those still only desire it to devote it to some noble enterprise, the exiguity of their resources not permitting them to manage it in person. Finally, a large number see in it chiefly a means of immediate gratification; but all, including those who hold positions whether in the liberal pro-

fessions or in the commercial world—artists,
artizans, proprietors, all who are capable of
earning ready money may have their work
classed under the denomination of business.

A business, in whatever category it belongs,
demands for success many qualities, among
which strength of character takes first rank.
This latter is a weapon of defense against the
worst temptations. It gives its skilful possessor
a superiority over his opponents that is incontestable. Strength of character, destined to
triumph in the kingdom of business, is composed
of special qualities, chief of which is coolness of
temperament, which proceeds from self-possession. With certain people this coolness of temperament is of a moderate cast and takes the
name of phlegm.

Phlegm is a defense against visible emotion.
It is not hypocrisy or falsehood, for the phlegmatic utter no sentiment contrary to that which
they fill. They are content not to let anything
transpire of the causes of their agitation. One
may compare a phlegmatic man to a thick veil
under which the play of the features, and under
this the acts of the mind, are dissembled.

Hypocrisy resembles a dead wall covered with
lying advertisements.

II.8

Phlegm is this dead wall wholly denuded of these. We can conjecture what it conceals, but in no case can we accuse it of saying anything contrary to truth.

Coolness of temperament, too often confounded with phlegm, differs from it in the sense that it is in need of some special circumstance for its manifestation. It is founded above all in quick decision, the result of brief deduction, of which the characteristics are prudence and just appreciation. In the ordinary circumstances of life coolness of temperament is known as circumspection.

Circumspection is very precise in its affairs. It is a quality that draws its origin from strength of character, for it goes straight to its desired object. Thanks to circumspection one will avoid pronouncing upon a thing until he has made a thorough study of it in its possible combinations. Further, it is the trait that supplies the necessary clearness requisite to guaranty engagements made beforehand by furnishing pretexts for momentary abstention, if such be profitable for the business in hand.

And since we have made use of the word clearness, let us say something about its concern in business affairs.

It is the gift that permits us to foresee the consequences of the act dictated by coolness of temperament. Clearness can not exist without strength of character, for it is the latter which supplies the will-power essential to getting rid of the burdensome considerations that keep us from discussing the right course.

Clearness is like a light brought into the midst of darkness; as the illumination permits of distinguishing each object lost in shadow, clearness shows all the motives detaching themselves from the mists of the principal theme, no matter how involved. In case of possible disaster it will show in a strong light the disadvantages of some act that may be fatal, tho it seem to us beneficent. It is above all a preventive quality; it does not determine, it points out, and thus serves to caution us against possible impending danger.

Before seizing an object we direct toward it and what surrounds it the rays of the lamp, examining everything in the light. And when we have fixt our choice we like to convince ourselves by means of minute scrutiny that it is worth while.

Here ends the rôle of clearness, whose place is now taken by perspicacity.

This is the quality that permits of discerning the real value of the object, or its utility.

Prudence now intervenes in order to permit us to envisage the disadvantages incurred in the resolution.

Discernment will enable us to see the advantages that may flow from it.

Reason provides us with the faculty of comparing and weighing these advantages to the end that we may know exactly which to choose.

Deduction permits us to infer their consequences, the probability of which will be in accordance with the strictness of the mental operation.

Finally, coolness of temperament, the synthesis of all these qualities, will appear upon the scene to aid us to put in practise the resolutions they have inspired.

These resolutions may be important or simply may concern the humblest questions of daily life; they will exhibit an intimate relation with coolness of temperament.

Strength of character will be found valuable in that it will put the lid down upon the effervescence of those who waste themselves in words. Such as these give copious utterance to puerile wishes, but miscarry lamentably when it is a

question of making them good. Others allow
themselves to be carried away by a too-apparent
frankness and are incapable of that urbanity
which is the necessary condition of carrying on
all business.

Urbanity can be practised in all circumstances of social life. It consists in a form of
politeness which by no means excludes firmness,
but has a way of recovering it agreeably. It is
suggestive of the well-known image of the iron
hand in a velvet glove. By using politeness it
is possible to refuse what is injurious to our
interests without hurting the one we address.

Urbanity is the brilliant covering of the
bitter pill. We are all made so that an insipid
medicament presented to us in pleasant guise
has more attraction for us than has some dainty
of repulsive aspect.

Strength of character in business is the appanage of those who are accustomed to call in
logic in their decisions; which decisions being
unembarrassed by the feeble sentiment that is
characteristic of the weak, always bear the ear-
mark of truth.

In cultivating logic, that is to say the art of
reasoning, there is less chance of being deceived
and precious time is saved, for he who gives

himself up to tergiversations may be regarded in the light of a spendthrift. Moreover, those who cultivate logic, by compelling their minds to the exercise of thought soon become of the class known as prudent. The habit of rapid reflection opens to them horizons that must always remain cloud to those of feeble will, with the result that they can always create for themselves opportunities of wide import. They are the sort of whom it is said, "everything succeeds with them."

One might add that if success comes to them it is because they know how to gain and keep it themselves instead of uncomfortably waiting for it to come from some one else.

CHAPTER IV

STRENGTH OF CHARACTER IN EVERY-DAY LIFE

INDIVIDUAL happiness is always in direct ratio to the efforts made to obtain it. Discipline, self-control, the awakening in ourselves of the proper condition of mind to attain to success in our pursuits—these in brief *résumé* constitute the chief desire of all.

All do not use the same formula in their aspirations. But there is no one that does not tend more or less actively toward some achievement. This achievement may consist of a series of accomplishments all of which concur to produce the general end in view; at times, however, it is a question of but one decisive act from which should flow some profitable result. In daily life, moreover, the first case is the most frequent one, the second coming solely as an exception.

It is rarely needful to enter upon a grave resolution, but we should in the day's course re-

117

solve on a series of minute determinations whose multiplicity constitutes the directing force.

For a woman the education of her children, their maintenance, the cares of the home, the ordering of meals, surveillance of servants and their maintenance and wages are all occasions for developing qualities of patience, perseverance, judgment and perspicacity, all of which constitute strength of character.

Upon the accomplishment of these obscure duties depend most often the peace and harmony of life. They have a preponderant influence upon a man's state of mind; for accordingly as he is well or badly served, accordingly as the character of his surroundings is congenial or otherwise, he will come to love or dislike his home. Outside of internal disputes that trouble the existence of all who have to undergo them, there is a species of constant agitation that disposes us to unreasonable nervousness and interferes seriously with our duties. Strength of character banished from the home relinquishes it to reasonless impulsiveness, which then comfortably installs itself, bringing in its train the procession of disagreements and moral disorders, upon which sane reason, tossed about and buffeted from all sides, quickly makes its escape without intending to return.

Veracity, integrity, and goodness, which form the essence of strong character, do not find themselves at ease among acts that lack reflection.

Firmness of purpose is a power that can be exercised as well in the ordinary acts of life as in those inspired by circumstances of grave nature. All educators ought to let this truth sink into their minds.

The education that tends to moral virility is a question of example. Children always adopt the character and ways of those who direct them. Even in cases where they are rebellious they always incline to introduce into the very contradictions they fight for the elements and ways of life that they have learned from their teacher. Example is one of the most real instructors that it is possible to conceive of; its silent and persistent power betrays itself in habits of mind, unconscious at times, which blends the life of pupil and master in such community of thought and feeling that it is always difficult to change it.

It is therefore indispensable to give to children from early youth principles of strong character which later on will be seen to develop to advantage. And to fortify the lesson example is invaluable.

It is apparent how strength of character in parents can influence children for good. It may transform their whole life by arming them against deceptions and reverses. Often it prevents misfortune from coming; but even in case of its arrival those who have been brought up in the school of strong principle will know how to accept it without weakness.

This firmness of character will prevent many a disaster in the morning of life; it will prove to be a barrier against the allurements at the bottom of which is found nothing but disappointment and disgust, and will enable counsels of reason to prevail with those whom the impetuosity of twenty-one may have led into the pathways frequented by vice.

Later on it will again intervene, the time having come to make choice of a career. It is then that strength of character becomes an office of daily application. The principal effort resolved upon, the career chosen, the grave resolution taken, it becomes a question of "making good." Only feeble spirits are content to look upon the bright side of what attracts them. Strong characters take a kind of delight in stripping the object of desire of all ornament that may give it an aspect foreign to its nature. For these last there are therefore less deceptions; deceptions nevertheless will present themselves in goodly number and it is the part of strength of character to palliate them rather than have recourse to dissimulation.

Later on choice of a companion for the voyage of existence will give occasion for the developing of those sturdy qualities that should animate us all. Here sane reason should impose its laws upon us and it will be well to recall the celebrated axiom:

"It is not by the ornaments at the ship's prow that the passengers are assured of safety."

There are cases where strength of character should lend us its powerful aid to resist the physical allurements that conceal moral defects.

Stoicism is not limited to contempt for physical suffering; at times it consists in the resolve to endure suffering of sentimental nature, the cause of which seems an unworthy one. Further, it is character that equips us with the strength to resist passions of small, demeaning nature, which at the turning-point of forty often assail those who have succeeded in warding them off in their youth.

Every one may be master of himself, but the law involves a different interpretation for each.

The exigencies of life demand from each one a different effort. An artizan can not be expected to do the work of a magistrate; a musician or a literary worker can not have the mind of a man who deals in realities dependent upon material effort.

There is a marked difference between the laws of reality and the laws of thought, considered in an ideal aspect. Nevertheless, the laws of this same thought, made up of true elements whence flow firm and directed determination, are valid for all.

We know that all contradictory judgments are tainted with falsehood. Weakness of character has the effect always of maiming reason, with the consequent result of producing contradictory decisions. It also engenders that pitiful means of defense, falsehood. Weak characters are rarely immune from this. It is a sort of necessity for them; it is the way they remedy or think they remedy the insufficiency of their means of defense. Lack of intelligence does not permit them to appreciate the consequences incurred by their want of frankness. It is more difficult to support a falsehood than to face the risks of truth.

The habit of frankness permits of viewing an event in all its phases and of guarding against painful surprizes. It is to be remarked that liars are seldom in good faith with themselves. The habit of perverting truth makes them less delicate in regard to sincerity in general. Also it is not a rare thing to see liars dupe themselves involuntarily just as they consciously seek to dupe others. This habit is in every-day life the cause of frequent disorders, and constant disputes. The custom of dissembling everything always proceeds from weakness of character which thinks thus to suppress difficulties. The liar does not reflect that the fact of destroying certain obstacles by the word does not prevent them from subsisting in reality, and that the desired ignorance in which it is sought to keep the interested makes them neglect the necessary precautions for their safety. Proneness to lying in the little incidents of daily life has its source in two opposite sentiments, both of which proceed from weakness of character. The first is the strong desire to play a part. One who is possest with this, not feeling in himself the strength of will that gives the necessary aptitude for great results, transforms for his own benefit everything that he

comes in contact with. He appears on the scene,
looks around, takes in everything, and speaks
his thoughts. Very well; these things are always to his advantage, and he always over-
whelms his hearers with the idea of his importance. The whole thing usually ends most piti-
fully for the deceiver, his deceptions always
being quickly discovered.

The other sentiment consists in mental idleness which looks with horror upon every sort
of complication, even the most insignificant.
Weaklings who are afflicted with this defect will
lie to escape the slightest trouble.

A young man given to lying, a weakling, was
sent by his father to get some information from
his former employers concerning one about to
be engaged. Instead of taking the usual measures the young man found it more simple to
give his father excellent recommendations which
the latter did not think of verifying. Some
months later a deficit in the accounts attracted
his attention; the employees were watched, and
it was found the newcomer was the author of
the thefts. Imagine the agitation of the father,
who, before taking stern measures, demanded an
interview with the delinquent's former employers
who had so cheerfully given excellent references.

Great was his stupefaction on learning that they had discharged this employee for cause and had never heard any more about him, much less given him references.

Habitual lying has not always such grievous immediate results as this, but it has another kind that is not less reprehensible; it creates mistrust and destroys confidence, upon which harmony is based. With doubt is born a sort of contempt for the person in whose word it is impossible to trust.

In time, discredit attaints his very nature and it becomes impossible for him to give his mind to any real achievement, all the more because he does not know the value of noble things and no longer wants to be of those who live in the light of day, and whose reliance is placed upon truth and character without which no enterprise can have hope of success.

CHAPTER V

HAPPINESS AND STRENGTH OF CHARACTER

IT is an absurd theory which places happiness in an effortless life.

Each one here below has his formula, and it is long indeed since the sage uttered this thought: "What makes the happiness of one does not at all make that of another."

The meaning of the maxim has been trusted by those who like to see in it a sort of *revanche* of fate by which some are permitted to profit at the expense of others. We should like to believe that the author of this proverb has really deserved the title of thinker and that he only desired to express this fact: "The conception of happiness is not the same for all."

There are those whose ambition is limited by a life of peace and harmony. Others crave brilliant triumphs and find happiness in honor and wealth alone. For certain persons honors and brilliant existence are the sole desirable aim. To reach the height of these diverse am-

bitions but one means exists—conquest. In
order to conquer there is but one means avail-
able, strength of character, which gives the will-
power to conquer. By virtue of strength of
character we may solve the problem of happy
labor which for nine-tenths of us means contentment. We have seen in a preceding chapter
that everybody, under one form or another, is
obliged to do some kind of work. Formerly
sovereigns with their ministers worked just like
artizans. All depended upon manual labor, all
worked and had to work.

Work done in a sullen way doubles the difficulty of effort, making it so hard at times that
we hesitate to attempt it. Gayety, the offspring
of character, gives elasticity to the mind and
lessens the sense of difficulty. Work done sul-
lenly is nearly always unproductive, and in-
sipidity of effort supervenes disagreeably upon
the ordinary conditions of happiness. To do
what has to be done with cheerfulness and to
apply oneself to it earnestly is the secret of
all felicity. If we are not careful the little
ennuis of life, untransformed by intelligent
action, end by invading our very lives and
leaving no place for joy to penetrate. They are
like fine flakes of snow which separately have no

consistency, dissolving as quickly as they fall, but whose accumulation means insuperable obstacles and even formidable avalanches.

Herein is exprest the trait of those who are ignorant of strength of character; they allow themselves to be dominated by the trifling bustle of daily life instead of transforming it by a use of will-power into events whose ordered course might give a vivid interest to daily life.

The essential condition of happiness consists above all in the power of willing it.

We do not mean to assert that the mere desire to be happy smoothes over all difficulties and does away with all the unpleasantness of life. But he who encourages his own life with a will for happiness always discovers in it reasons for contentment which hitherto have escaped his observation. We say *his own life* and not that of others. There is no more certain sign of feeble character than is the propensity to regard another's lot preferable to one's own. If the comparison is made in good faith it will generally be found that a grievous mistake has been made, and that to exchange some good of our own for that of our neighbor would be a bad bargain.

Happiness, moreover, is a question of relativity. In order to appreciate it we must take account of origin, habits, situation, age, etc. What makes for the happiness of a young man would be a matter of indifference to a man of maturity, while an old man will find pleasure in occupations that leave the latter indifferent. What would seem like want to a man used to wealth would appear like a desirable competence to a man unspoiled by it. Finally idleness, the avowed aim of so much effort, becomes for the one who realizes it a source of *ennui* bordering on sadness. Those who are endowed with strength of character are never ignorant of the fact; happiness is everywhere if one knows the secret of placing it in the accomplishment of a task.

Idleness, by annihilating desire, destroys interest in life. It is an unfailing source from which feeble souls draw the discouragement which makes them cry out on happiness; of such are the barren regrets concerning an act whose consequences can not be changed.

An Oriental proverb says: "It is better to yearn for a cabin than to mourn for a palace." And it is impossible not to admire the virile character of the mind that dictated the thought. Desire for a cabin implies a hard struggle to

II.10

possess one, a series of efforts that are necessary
to become its owner, a sustained daily interest
in the life of him who devotes himself to its
conquest. Regretting a palace amounts to an
avowal that we are reconciled to the fate that
has befallen us and are without hope of changing
it. The word barren as applied to regret is
no sterile phrase. Nothing can be more fruitless
than regrets. Nothing is more opposed to the
survival of happiness. He who calls himself
happy proclaims the plenitude of actual contentment and yet has hope of bettering his best.

But he who consumes himself in vain regret
gives the lie to the happiness of the magical
present and uses up his strength in deploring
conditions that nothing can change.

There is one circumstance, however, in which
regret may bear actual fruit. It is when we
call character to our aid in order to make a
thorough examination of the causes which have
provoked disaster. The examination may be
made by means of a single consideration; try
to discover the vice in the events which have
brought about the incident we deplore. If the
dénouement is due to lack of cleverness, to care-
lessness, or certain personal defects, regret for
them will not be fruitless, since they will in-

volve a resolution not to fall into the same errors a second time. There is no sense in regretting a past event unless we make a resolution not to relapse into the same faults which were produced by it.

Another cause of happiness is health.

Now health can not exist without strength of character, a quality which saves us from excess and enables us to take care of ourselves. No one will question that it is impossible to enjoy the happiness that life concedes us if suffering comes to spoil every hour. But are not we ourselves frequently the authors of this suffering?

Excess at table disposes some to ills of suggestion that poison their existence. Others consume their health in nightly fatigues and spend in sleep, often a besotted kind, the finest hours of the day, hours that seem to them insipid and disagreeable because they see them in the lens of their own lassitude. Others perhaps, suffer from some evil that the body ignores, but which, none the less, may be deep-seated.

Then there are the disillusioned, those who have demanded too much of happiness, and have not known enough to be content with what was given them. The trouble comes nearly always

from feebleness of character, which delights to
nourish itself with illusions whose false reflection dazzles them to the point of hiding from
them the necessity for effort. If they were
sincere they would confess that the poverty of
the result is in direct proportion to the energy
expended. All realization, barring unforeseen
accidents, responds exactly to the sum of activity deployed.

To this must be joined cleverness, however.
And this is still dependent upon strength of
character. A plan, to be well conceived, demands attention, analysis and good sense. How
can these be expected of one so weak as not to
be able to endure the thought of assiduity? It
is only persons of strong will-power who devote
to the elaboration of a task the amount of moral
and physical activity that it requires. Thus
they are rarely seen to become victims of the
shameful conclusions that the weak know too
well. They are not indeed under the wing of
that unforeseen felicity that is so seldom known,
but this kind of happiness is the exception, and
it must have been in alluding to people of character that one who had achieved distinguished
success remarked:

"We have the happiness that we deserve."

www.ingramcontent.com/pod-product-compliance
Lightning Source LLC
LaVergne TN
LVHW011205080426
835508LV00007B/612